1

Food came from animals and plants.

3

Emu eggs were eaten as a food.

Lizards were eaten as food.

7

A spear was thrown. It had to be very fast.

9

Kangaroos were hunted with spears.

11

You had to be very quiet and hide.

13

Dugongs were speared from a canoe.

Ducks were caught in lakes and ponds.

17

The tracks made by the animals were followed.

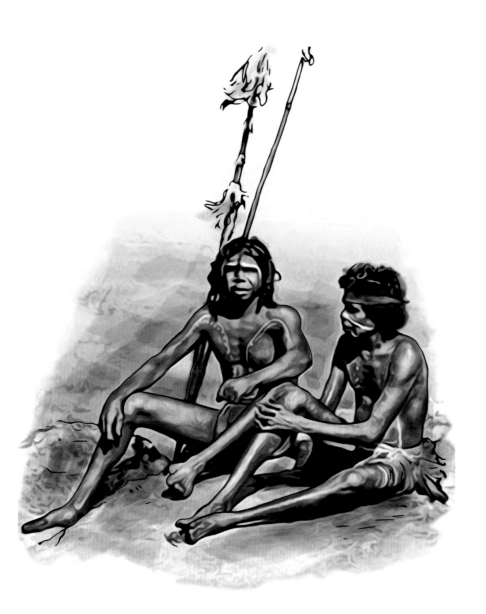

19

The ducks flew into the nets.

21

Spear tips were made very sharp.

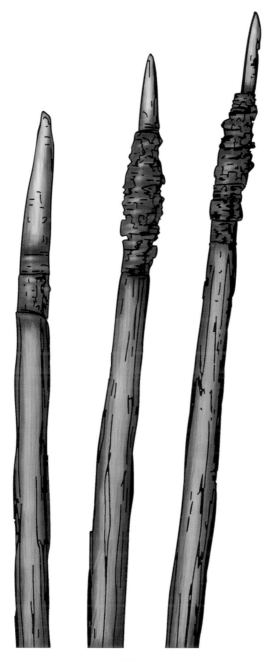

23

Word bank

food

animals

plants

emu

lizards

spear

kangaroos

quiet

dugong

canoe

eaten

tracks

followed

sharp